ISLAND MEMORIES: MY LIFE IN TRINIDAD

By Phyllis T. Nash-Lewis

Washington, D.C.

COVER INSPIRED

BY PHYLLIS T. NASH-LEWIS

Order this book online at www.trafford.com
or email orders@trafford.com

Most Trafford titles are also available at major online book retailers.

Printed in Victoria, BC, Canada.

ISBN: 978-1-4269-0758-6

Our mission is to efficiently provide the world's finest, most comprehensive book publishing service, enabling every author to experience success. To find out how to publish your book, your way, and have it available worldwide, visit us online at www.trafford.com

Trafford rev. 4/8/2010

 www.trafford.com

North America & international
toll-free: 1 888 232 4444 (USA & Canada)
phone: 250 383 6864 ♦ fax: 812 355 4082

ISLAND

MEMORIES

MY LIFE IN TRINIDAD

PREFACE

"Island Memories" is very interesting. It tells a story of a young girl growing up in the country on the Island of Trinidad with her nine siblings. Her Father was a farmer and her Mother a Housekeeper. While remembering her past, she became inspired by her Ancestors and those who she was associated with in her childhood days.

This book will be of interest to all generations.

Island Memories is also a challenge to others to start similar projects.

DEDICATION

I dedicate my first book to my grandchildren, Desiree, Tavaun, Victoria, Destiny, Denisha, Desmond and to all my future generations. I also dedicate this book to all my great Nieces and Nephews, too many names to mention.

Thanks to my grandmother Josephine, affectionately called Ma-me-me; you are gone but not forgotten. Your love for God has given me strength. My deepest, deepest gratitude to my parents, Darius and Paulina Thomas for their hard work, dedication and love in the upbringing of all their nine children. Thanks for giving us the discipline and rich culture that we will carry with us forever.

ACKNOWLEDGEMENTS

To my children, Tony, Tauna and Jason, thanks for accepting me as I am. I hope that you will be inspired by my history as I have been inspired by my parents. I love you all and may God bless and keep you in the right path always.

My deepest gratitude to my brother Mayhue who always believed in me and never stopped asking me for my book. To my nephew Randy, who after reading my letters, whenever I write to him, would say, "Aunty, why don't you write a book?" Thanks to my other brothers and sisters: Rupert, Ellis, Petty, Wallis, Eastlyn, Cecil and Urcilla. You all have given me the richness of my childhood days.

To my cousins from the front, Prowler, Charlo, Sub, Max, Margaret and Knolly, who visited us almost each and every day, you have all inspired me to write this book. To my cousins down the road, Ladyno, Tony, Janet, Carter and all others, I say thanks for the memories.

Thanks to all my cousins who came to visit our Grandmother, Ma-me-me bringing their children to play with us. Thanks to my two admirers, Rita who brought some of her nine children, Lynette and Mercha and Verona who also brought her boys, Kerr and Bryan to see ma-me-me. It was also a joy seeing Mary with some of her nine children and her sister Adlain and sometimes cousin Annesie with their mother, Tanty Cyril coming all the way from the city of Port of Spain or the town of San Fernando to see their mother, grandmother, sister and aunt.

Thanks to the Gasparillo crew, Cousin Vickey, Vanessa and Mertle with some of their children, Curley, Mervin, Randolph, Esther, Ann, Bernadette and the Stephens- Jeanette and Ms. Stephen. Most of all, thanks to Limers Club "too many names to mention", for giving me the unforgettable times of my youth and teaching me about their sports.

Thanks also to my niece, Kerine, for encouraging me to take the job at Howard University as a Secretary in the History Department, even though I had another job lined up.

SPECIAL ACKNOWLEDGEMENT

Working along with all the Professors and Students in the History Department at Howard University inspired me to write my own History. Thanks to Dr. David DeLeon for looking over my writings and telling me that it could be put into a book. Thanks to Dr. Quito Swan also for correcting some of my errors and congratulating me for my good work; and thanks to Craig Schiffert, PhD student in History, for copyediting my manuscript and making me believe that it is a writing project and I could complete and make it into a book.

This book could not be complete without the input of my eldest brother Rupert, who took time off his busy schedule to complete the editorial process, line by line, to get it ready to be published. Thanks to my neice Tricia Wallacia for putting my writings into this book format.

Contents

CHAPTER 1:
TRINIDAD

Trinidad is an island of about 1,860 square miles in the Caribbean Sea, near the coast of South America. Today the nation's population is approximately 1.3 million, mainly of African and East Indian origin, but also about five percent Chinese, Lebanese, European and American. People on the Island have always enjoyed the slow pace of life with its rich culture and diverse heritage. The Island's earliest settlers were Arawaks, who were followed by the Caribs.

When Columbus arrived on the Island in 1498, he gave it the name "Trinidad" ~the island with three hills. The Spanish settled in Sangre Grande, in the East, and San Fernando, in the south of the Island. Later, the French planters uprooted by the Haitian Revolution of 1789 gave us Sans Souci, Blanchisseuse and Matelot in the North and a couple other areas in the South. Finally, the British settled on the island, along with its sister island Tobago and it became a British crown colony.

Trinidad is also called, the "Land of the Hummingbird". The Scarlet Ibis with its shiny red color is another bird that is very famous on the island.

There are also many species of butterflies especially near plants with tropical flowers.

The Steeldrum was originated in Trinidad and made its own melodious music which became popular in every community on the island. Trinidadians made their own music like the calypso, soca and parang which is a Spanish version of celebration Christmas and other forms of music.

CHAPTER 2: RELIGION

There is a diversity of religions in Trinidad, which includes Christian Churches, Hindu Temples and Muslim Mosques. Spiritual ceremonies include Christian baptism, baptizing in the sea and the rivers, and the thunderous ceremonies of the Orisha, the Spiritual Baptist, an African faith transported throughout the Diaspora by the Yoruba people. The majority of the people on the Island are Christians and about twenty-five percent other religions.

One group is the "Jehovah Witness'" who went house-to-house preaching about the Bible and telling us that the world is coming to an end. They always came around in two's or in a group on Sundays when they knew most families would be at home. Even when my mother told them that her family was Catholic and did not wish to discuss religion, they still insisted that they listen. When they did not get anyone to listen to them, they would leave you a little leaflet.

Another group was the "Spiritual Baptists". There was a Baptist group about a half-mile from us in another village. Once a year they set up a tent next to their house and celebrated their faith, by giving a thanksgiving feast. Every night for one week there was praying and dancing. The group served different foods to everyone who wanted to eat. The participants were mainly middle-aged women and a few men. The women were usually dressed in white with their heads wrapped in their favorite colors. Most of the men beat the drums and sang African songs while the women danced to the beat.

I was told that the drums woke up their ancestors. The louder they beat, the quicker the women would get the spirit (power), while the crowd sang and clapped. Some of them would dance with something on their head, mainly a calabash or bowl. After catching the spirit, some of them would be healers, teachers or other professions in the spirit, while others traveled in their spirit to their ancestors' villages.

The "Hindu" religion is unique and mainly of East Indian descent. Some of the older men wore a white loincloth (doti) and the older women wore "saris" (long shiny chiffon scarves) and they spoke in Hindi. Some of them who were strong in their faith had sacred trees planted on the side of their homes or religious sites and temple grounds and sometimes they would have a lighted Deya (a small ceramic bowl with a candle) by the tree. It was also fun to go to East Indian weddings and witness the traditions of their Hindu faith. The Hindus would have arranged marriages where the bride and groom would see each other for the first time, during the wedding ceremony. It was their tradition also, for each side of the family to present gifts to the bride and groom at that time.

The "Anglican" and the "Roman Catholic" faiths, are somewhat similar to each other. Both faiths give communion during Mass. The bread and wine represent the body and blood of Our Lord Jesus Christ. The Island's Catholic training center is located on a mountain in the northern part of the island - Mount St. Bennedict. Young men, who want to join the priesthood or young women, who want to be a nun would be trained there.

Many churches and schools would have pilgrimages and retreats to the Mount. Other Catholics and some people of other faiths would join long lines to visit the Roman Catholic Church at the top of a mountain. Many people would go to get counseling from a priest or just to get a blessing; others would offer prayers of thanksgiving. Some believed in making penance by walking the two to three miles up to the Mount or just to go there to see the distant views of the beautiful island below the mountain.

CHAPTER 3: SEASONS

In Trinidad, there are two seasons: Rainy season and Dry season. Dry season used to be called "Crop Time" by the locals.

Rainy season starts with a holiday on the Island which is "Corpus Christi," a time when the Catholic Church celebrates the Body of Christ. Rainy season, from around June to December, is also a time when farmers begin to plant their crops. Sometimes, the sun came out so bright as though trying to burst from the clouds–and then suddenly the sky would turn dark and we knew that it was about to rain.

At this time, people hurried up to take their clothes off their clotheslines. Farmers rushed home from their gardens and children who were playing outside would run to their homes because they never knew how long or how heavy the rain would fall. Thunder begins to rumble and the rain would come pounding down to the ground. Sometimes when lightening accompanied the thunder, the flashes would be so bright through the windows in the house that you would duck for cover.

Then there was the earthquake and the house would begin to shake so hard that items would fall of the shelves in our home and mother would tell us children to get down on our knees and pray. When there was very heavy rain, the rivers overflowed their banks and water would come up to the steps of some of the houses. It was a beautiful sight to see the sun coming out right after the rain and the multicolor rainbow stretching from the sky to the rivers as we, the children, played in the flooded waters and bathed in the rain. My mother would fill her jugs with rain water for drinking and she made sure that the barrels were also filled for washing or emergency purposes.

Dry season or "Crop time" is around January to May, when the farmers reap their crops. Like rainy season, sometimes the sun would be so bright as though trying to burst from the clouds--and then sink slowly back at night. During Crop time it was hot, but the wind made living more comfortable on the Island. The farmers in my village were anxiously getting their sugarcane ready for the sugar mill. The roads were busy with mule carts, donkey carts and trucks taking the sugarcane to the mill in Forest Park village to grind and to be made into sugar and rum.

CHAPTER 4: CARNIVAL

Carnival in Trinidad is considered by many as the greatest in the world. The steel pan music is one of the main attractions of the carnival-- especially when followed by the masqueraders in the parade. Sometimes, the un-amplified melody of the pan is drowned by the loudspeakers on the music trucks that carry other conventional musical instruments. Carnival is celebrated on the two days just before the start of the Lenten season on Ash Wednesday, and everyone who wants can participate by paying a small fee for the costumes or just to play in a band. Politicians, social workers, teachers, and locals who love to have fun and free-up themselves can participate. It is also an educational event, when school children compete for prizes by entering into the calypso competition and the kiddies carnival.

Masqueraders celebrate for two days non-stop with beautiful costumes representing history of olden days; parading on the streets of the cities in different bands, some with many colorful sections. During carnival time, each band is followed by either a steel band or an instrumental band playing the sweet sounds of Trinidad calypso music. In the six to nine weeks prior to carnival, there are parties, shows and other entertainments leading up to Carnival Monday morning when thousands participate in J'ouvert "parading on the streets" in the early hours of the morning. Prizes are given to the best masquerade bands and best individual costumes.

Carnival Monday evening, many masqueraders are tired but still participate in the events. A number of bands from different villages and towns that take part in the various competitions around the island are judged by their costumes and their music. The calypso that is played most at these competitions is judged the best "road march" tune and its singer receives a grand prize.

Carnival Tuesday is the main event and the last day before Lent when people can jump up on the streets and parade in their costumes. It is the big day, when all the registered bands turn out in full splendour, reminding one of history, each band with a King and Queen leading them in the parade and wearing different historical costumes, each competing for an annual crown and valuable prizes.

Some bands have young children also and then there are some independent groups like the Moko-Jumbie (someone walking on stilts making him ten to fifteen feet tall) and the Jab-Jab, which had something to do with slavery, participating in the revelry by parading in the band of their choice. Carnival Tuesday is also a time when a large number of tourists travel from other countries to Trinidad to see the greatest show on earth--and some even to play mas in the band of their choice.

Author and friends

CHAPTER 5:
MY CHILDHOOD

I was born in Union Village, Claxton Bay, in the Southern part of the Island of Trinidad shortly after World War II began. I know that because my mother talked endlessly about the war and giving birth to her new baby, which is me. I am the fourth of ten children. My mother talked about the American base which was situated in Port of Spain, the capital of Trinidad which is in the North of the Island. She also spoke of the handsome young American military men who came to the city during their off days. They were called Yankees by some of the locals .

My mother also remembered the hard times in the island during the war. There was a shortage of food and people waited for hours in long lines to receive a ration card to buy basic groceries. My father was a farmer and had crops of vegetables and fruits. When there was no bread in the home, my father made corn porridge and we had slices of breadfruit for breakfast and sometimes cassava bread, all the produce coming from his garden. In spite of all the hardships, my parents survived the war.

CHAPTER 6: PARENTS

Both my mother and father were born in Claxton Bay. My mother was the last of nine girls. Her godparents lived in Belmont, a little town in the city of Port of Spain, and owned their home. They had no children so they asked my grandmother to adopt my mother as their godchild. My mother was happy to be with her new parents.

It was a big difference to her, coming from a large family in the country to live in the city with her godparents in their quiet home. She enjoyed the city life with the busy streets, and the big Savannah (park), which she walked around many times, with its cricket matches, soccer games, and other events. Some of the city's largest buildings surrounded the savannah and vendors lined the side streets selling coconut water, roast corns and other delicacies. My mother's adopted parents treated her as their own child and took her everywhere that they went, including some theatre shows and fairs.

Her new parents were considered middle class. Her stepfather was a Police Officer and her stepmother was a housewife. At that time, police officers were very much respected, even more than they are today. It was considered an excellent career path in the islands. In those days, most women stayed at home to do the housework and take care of their children. My mother's godparents had a large plantation of cocoa and coffee in a far away tiny village of Poole. Hired hands worked their crops. Cocoa was one of the biggest exports in Trinidad at the time.

My father was short, well-built and dark-skinned. He always said that he was strong and he had African blood in him because his forefathers were from Africa. He had three sisters and since he was the only son, he did all the manly work around the house, such as cleaning the yard and cutting wood for fire and helping his father in the garden.

I never knew my grandparents on my father's side. My father talked about them so much, however, that I felt as if I did know them. My father said that his great-great- grandparents came from Africa on a boat and his great-great-grandmother turned into a mermaid and returned to Africa. To this day, I wonder if it's true. He also said that his grandfather's name was Gwama Guez, meaning "strong man".

My grandfather was called Papa by everyone in the family. He was a farmer and worked very hard to support his family. My father loved his home, which he called Papa's house. The house sat on a little hill, about twelve feet off the main road. There was a small river flowing just below the hill at the back of the house where my parents drew water for domestic purposes. That river has since dried into rocks and grass. Beyond the river from Papa's house were acres of land and most of it was planted with sugar cane and a smaller part with fruit trees.

Mother spoke endlessly about growing up with her adopted parents. She was not allowed to go to the fields to work. She was driven wherever she went. She occasionally visited her birth mother in the country, but she was now a city girl and loved it. She always told us that her marriage was arranged. Her father had passed on and her mother was getting older so she wanted to see her youngest child get married and settled down before she died. Her adopted parents could not convince my grandmother to let my mother stay in the city and marry someone there. My maternal grandmother knew my father's family and knew that my father was a hard-working young man of a decent family. She was determined to have my mother married to my father. The two families got together, discussed their children's future, and a wedding resulted.

"My grandmother lived to be over one hundred years old".

My parents had a big wedding. The family, friends and relatives of both the bride and groom gathered together to witness the ceremony. My mother spoke of the grand wedding that they had. She cherished her wedding gifts and only used them on special occasions. She also spoke of the two wedding dresses that she got, one each from her mother and her godparents. She wore one on the wedding day and the other on the following Sunday. Typically, the second Sunday after a wedding was a large gathering where families and friends of both bride and groom became acquainted.

After the marriage, my mother moved from the City of Port of Spain to live with my father, her husband, in Papa's house in a little village called Caratal. This was a small farming community where most of the villagers were of East Indian descent and lived in mainly small homes or huts covered with carat leaves (like the leaf of the palm tree). Some of the houses were built on posts; underneath was smooth pavement made with horse manure mixed with sand, which looked like cement.

As compared to the city, there were no street lights or electricity in the village and the houses were far apart from each other. Driving South on the main road from Claxton Bay, in the central part of Trinidad, you would first enter St. Margaret's village, then Union Village, where we grew up, and then arrive at Caratal. Claxton Bay is noted for its cement factory. Cement made here is shipped throughout the Caribbean and is also used locally. Claxton Bay farmers grew lots of sugarcane which was taken during Crop Time to the Forres Park Cane Factory to be ground and made into sugar, molasses and rum. The Forres Park factory was to the east of Claxton Bay. Trinidad is also known for producing Angostura bitters, which is used by most people in the country to flavor foods and drinks.

It was a big adjustment for my mother in Papa's house. She had to use oil lamps or a flambeau (a bottle with kerosene and a wick which was used as a flashlight) to go to the latrine (outhouse) at night. She kept a posy (a night bowl) under her bed for any emergency. She hated the nights in the country because she could hear frogs, night birds and owls howling near Papa's house. My father never complained because he was used to living there. Still, my father did everything to make his new wife comfortable. He even bought a net (canopy) to put over the bed so that mosquitoes or flies could not come near while she was asleep.

It was a few years later that Papa died of complications from a train accident in which he suffered a broken leg. My mother then told my father that she wanted to move to Union Village, nearer to her mother, sister and other relatives, since it was a more populated area and closer to the City, the elementary school and the village standpipe (a public water supply), which was directly across the street from her mother's house and you can even walk to the sea (beach). Union Village was also closer to the town of San Fernando in the South of Trinidad and therefore easier to get transportation.

My maternal grandmother was named Josephine, but everyone called her Ma-me-me. Ma-me-me's house stood on about an acre of church land. Most of the land in Union Village was owned by the Anglican Church. Everyone who had houses on this land had to pay a small yearly rental tax. Since the houses in Union were closer to each other than in Caratal, most of the people knew each other. My parents did not have to walk a mile to get water as they had done in Caratal. Standpipes provided a free public water supply and was the main source of water for many villages. People would wait in line with their buckets to get water for their use.

In our home at Union Village, a river also ran about two hundred yards from the back of the house, and yards from that river was a sand quarry where trucks from other parts of the country came to purchase loads of sand for construction purposes. The quarry was like a little mountain of sand and trucks were lined up with their own laborers to shovel the sand and fill their trucks.

Yards away from the sand quarry stood a water-well with a spring emerging from the earth. People went there to draw water for bathing, washing and (after it was boiled) drinking. A bucket was lowered into the well with a chain to fetch the water and each person, mainly women, stood in line with their buckets. That area is now a savannah or park called "The Spring" and is the home of Union Village Community Center, which serves the same purpose even today.

My mother had asked her mother if my father could build a little house at the back of hers until they could do better. At that time, Ma-me-me lived with one of her daughters, Nen, who had three sons. Her eldest son lived with his father in another town. Two of Ma-me-me's granddaughters, Rita and Margaret, whose mother was deceased, also came to live with them at a very young age. They all lived in a two-room house. My mother was happy and she told my father that her mother had approved of them moving to Union Village.

My father was also overjoyed, because he too was happy to move closer to the town and a more populated area, and nearer to his wife's relatives. He immediately started packing and getting wood and coconut branches from his garden to build his new house. Carat branches were used for the roof and he used the sand-and-manure cement to construct the walls. With some help from the villagers, my father built a two-room house attached to the back of my grandmother's, and my parents and their young children at the time moved into their new house in Union village. My mother could not be happier to be near her natural mother, her sister and other relatives who lived a few miles down the road. All the children enjoyed playing together.

CHAPTER 7:
SCHOOL DAYS

The elementary school, Union Presbyterian School, was and still is the only elementary school in the village. It was about five minutes away from our house. On the way to school there was a river that ran below the road and the bridge was made with white iron rail. It was the same river that ran all through the village. With its white iron railing, the bridge became a landmark to the school and the village people, and is called "The Bridge" even today.

The Presbyterian Church was next to the school. Most of the kids who attended the school lived in the village, while about ten percent attended private schools out of the area. The school bell rang about ten minutes before class started on mornings, so my mother would let us leave home just after the bell rang. Most times, my cousins and brothers waited for some of their friends to walk to school together.

Our school had two levels. There were no walls dividing the classrooms. The classes from first through third primer (grade) were on the lower level, and the first standard through seventh standard on the top level. The stage was at the head of the school and the Headmaster's desk was in the corner of the stage overlooking all the classes. The school-children wore blue uniforms and the teachers who were mainly men wore white or light-blue shirts and dark colored pants.

Every morning, before going to our classrooms, we had to stand in line in the schoolyard, each class in a row from the lowest grade to the highest grade. We all said the Morning Prayer and then sang "God Save the Queen". Since the Island was a British colony at the time, it was a tradition for us to follow the British rules and Queen Elizabeth ruled at the time. While outside, the teachers would take a count of their classes then we would go to our classrooms.

Our school had one recess period in the morning and one in the afternoon. During recess, we got a chance to use the toilets and to play with our friends. Some of the children who lived far away and had an allowance would buy snacks from the vendors who were on the school grounds. They were mostly older women selling their homemade Island delicacies, like anchar, kurma, channa or chilibibi, which was always good to us. When it was lunch time, the children who lived far away would eat their home-prepared lunch in school. We who lived nearby would go home for lunch. Mother cooked everyday, so we always had a hot meal for lunch and we knew when to go back to school when we heard the school bell ring.

Our school sometimes took us on outings to visit the different geographical sites. The Pitch Lake was the most favorite site that I remembered visiting. It was the largest area of black pitch that I ever saw in one place. There were pools of water in some areas and it was always so clear that you can see the depth of it. Some areas had soft pitch, so it was off-limits, because a person might sink right in! Trucks from all over the country came to get pitch to pave their roads. Today, the Pitch Lake in La Brea has less pitch, but it is still one of Trinidad's biggest tourist attractions.

Another grand site was the Caroni River, in the Northern part of the country. It is the longest river in Trinidad. We also had the man-made Dry River, which was concrete at the bottom and the water ran through so fast that it always looked dry. It ran through the city of Port of Spain to the dock area and the Caribbean Sea. Our school also took us to the cloth factory to see how materials were made. It was always fun for us kids to go on school outings; for most of us, it was the only time that we would travel out the village.

I loved school, my teachers and my classmates. As far back as I can remember, I was in the top five of my class. I never liked Geography or History but I liked Math and English. We did not have "multiple choice" tests at that time, so you either knew the answer to the questions or you did not. I was shy and quiet, but eager to learn. My dream was to go to college and become a teacher.

CHAPTER 8: MY SIBLINGS

After my mother left the home of her adopted parents, she visited them occasionally. It was sad when she had to leave them to go home to her own family. About a year and a half after her first baby, Rupert, my mother had a second baby boy, Ellis. Two years later she became pregnant with another child, "Petty" so she decided to leave Rupert with her adopted parents because she knew that being with them, he would be well cared for. They decided to adopt my oldest brother so he grew up with them in the city of Port-of-Spain.

At that time, if girls became too old and were unmarried, they were called "Old Maids." I knew what my parents had in mind for me as I was getting older. They talked about me meeting a nice gentleman. My aunt, Tanty Vicky (my father's sister), would sometimes mention it. My father suggested that I learn to sew and become a seamstress like most of the young women in the village. I was not ready to get married and have lots of children. I told my father that I knew how to sew; he did not have to spend his money to send me to be a seamstress.

My mother had a sewing machine, so I would take my old clothes, cut them and make little dresses or take an old dress and make a skirt. I practiced and became better at sewing, but it was not what I wanted to do for a living. My mother decided to send me to her niece, my cousin Verona, a professional seamstress in another village, to learn to sew and help her out since she had many customers. There, I was able to learn a little, just enough to sew for myself.

My older brothers were now employed. While Ellis was in the Police Force, Rupert worked as a Clerk with the court system. A government job in those days was considered a good way to make a living, so my brothers thought that it was good for me to work for the Government. Most entry at that time jobs required typing.

My brothers knew that my parents could not afford to send me to college and that I was too young to get married, so they suggested that they would both pay for me to go to college. I said yes, I would love to go. They registered me at a commercial college where I also took shorthand

and typing. On the first day of school, I knew that I would like it. I graduated with high speed in both shorthand and typing. Later on, that paid off for me. I did not get a job with the Government but I worked with a private firm.

After leaving school, I became very active in the community and still did some of my regular chores. I joined the village council, where I was voted Secretary. I was proud of this since the Chairman, Mr. Marjadsingh, was the Headmaster of our elementary school. I was also the Secretary of the women's group for the village. At that time, there were a lot of young people in the country staying at home after school age; this was because some parents could not afford to send their children to college and there were not enough jobs available for the youths, so the Government came up with programs to help those young people who had finished school and were interested in some type of vocational training.

Most villages participated in the programs, and professional Instructors were paid to go out to the different communities to teach the youths and some adults in their villages. The courses were given once or twice a week. I took handicrafts and also the cooking course once a week in our community center. We were fortunate to have two of my mother's nieces, Cousin Vicky and Cousin Vanessa, as Instructors for our village. They traveled from the town of Gasparillo to Union Village, and they were always well-dressed and well-spoken, and even though we were cousins, I was treated like everyone else. We learned to crochet, knit and weave from banana leaves and coconut straw. We were given recipes to make dishes from scratch, and although I was never good at cooking, I kept my recipe book and still look at some of my recipes even today. We always had a big bash after the end of each program where we displayed all of our items and invited the people in the community.

CHAPTER 9: RECIPES

Here are some of my favorite recipes from yester-year.

Saltfish Pie

1 1b. saltfish soaked	3 tbsps milk
2 or 3 raw onions	4 tbsps bread crumbs
3 or 4 fresh tomatoes	11b. potatoes, boiled and sliced
11b. potatoes boiledmashed cream-style	

Method

Grease pie dish and at bottom put a layer of potatoes, saltfish, raw onion and another of tomatoes. Sprinkle with bread crumbs. Bake in moderate oven for 30 minutes.

Sahina-A-La-Creole

12 large dasheen (like spinach) leaves	1 cup flour
2 eggs	3 tsps salt
1 lemon or lime	Water to make a thin batter
1 tsp black pepper	

Method

Remove strings from leaves, wash well in water in which lemon or lime is squeezed. Handle leaves carefully to prevent them from tearing, then dry on kitchen towel. Make thin batter of remaining ingredients and spread it sparingly on the back of each leaf. Roll, slice, and fry.

And I loved the Peanut-butter drink.

Peanut Butter Drink

3 tbsps peanut butter	*1 pint milk*
*Sugar to taste_**or***	*1 cup hot water*
3 tsps of vanilla ice cream	*3 cups cold water*

Method

Pour hot water into mixing bowl, add cold peanut butter, dissolve for five minutes. Then add this mixture to the cold water, add milk, and sweeten to taste. Sprinkle a few drops of vanilla essence to your liking. Cool - Serve six people.

Coconut Raisin Pudding

3 eggs beaten	1 grated coconut
2 cups milk	4 oz. raisins chopped
4 oz. sugar	Pinch grated nutmeg

Method

Stir milk and sugar then add coconut, raisins, and beaten egg. Turn into well-greased dish and sprinkle with a little nutmeg, then bake at 350 degrees for 25 minutes.

CHAPTER 10: CHURCH

We attended the Roman Catholic Church that stands on a hill in the village of Pointe-a-Pierre which was nearer to the town of San Fernando. In the heart of Pointe-a-Pierre was Texaco's oil refinery. Oil is another of Trinidad's main products and is shipped to other Caribbean Islands and North America.

When we became of age, being of the Catholic faith, we made our first Communion and later prepared for Confirmation. It was the tradition for Christian parents in the Island to have their children confirmed around the age of twelve or at the end of elementary schooling. We had to study the Catholic faith to be confirmed, and go for instructions for at least six months. It was fun going on Saturdays with our cousins and some of our neighboring friends who were also of the Catholic faith.

The Author on her way from church wth her self made dress

Although it was a long walk from home to the Church, we never complained or felt tired. It was something that we knew we had to do. We always took the shortcut through the tracks (trails) of Monfan Hill to the village of Pointe-a-Pierre. On our way back from instructions, we would sometimes get mangoes from the trees near the track. There were different fruit trees along the path. The boys would climb the trees and shake the branches or pelt stones so the mangoes or other fruit would fall to the ground. We especially liked the "do-duce" mango because it was small and sweet. The "calabash" mango was also delicious and it was round and looked like a calabash; and the "starch" mango melted in your mouth. Then, there was the "julie" mango. "Umm." Sometimes, the boys had their slingshots with them. Usually, someone would stay on the side to watch for the property owners while we picked their fruits.

Another memorable time for me was November 1st of each year, which was "All Saints Day", a Christian tradition when most families would light candles on their ancestors' graves. The 2nd of November was called "All Souls Day", when Christian families would usually light candles on the front of their homes, on their galleries (porches) or front steps in remembrance of the dear ones who had passed on. It was always fun for us because we would go down the road to see how many candles each house would light. To us, it was like Christmas lights. My grandmother was famous for lighting a number of candles. She lit one for each of her kin who had died and she was then almost ninety years old.

I was encouraged to join the Legion of Mary, a Catholic group of women who went out to pray for the sick and shut-ins once every two weeks. It was a small group of about six adults and three teenagers, of which I was one. We attended meetings once a week after church on Sundays, usually for about an hour. We said the rosary and prayed for the sick and shut-ins, who could not attend church that week.

CHAPTER 11: SPORTS

One of our neighbors who had just moved to the village was a basketball coach. Mr. Cox wanted to put together a girl's basketball team, since we already had a team for "rounders," which is a ladies' game, except that we played the game just for fun. We now had a new girls' basketball team. I was a center-forward. Marjorie, who is my cousin, was also a favorite and the best on our team; she had long legs and when she got the ball, no one could catch up with her.

We played in the village and other counties on the Island. Mr. Cox saw how active we were, so he asked us to join the sports club where we were trained to run the 100- and 200-meter races and also the hurdles. We trained at the Texaco Oil Refinery's "park". I practiced hard to make the team. I entered one of the biggest games on the Island, which was called the Southern Games.

Representatives of the sports clubs in Trinidad and Tobago competed against each other and the winners represented the country. I won the 100-dash heat and was very excited to run on the day of the games. That was one of my special moments because I was representing my family and my village in the Southern Games. Everyone came out to cheer me. Although I did not qualify, I was overjoyed to hear everyone's voices calling me out and encouraging me to go on. When I finally got to the end of the line, I was so relieved and proud; I just waved to the crowd. That was my first and only professional sport for my country.

CHAPTER 12: "LUNCH"

Almost every Sunday, my father would go to the yard, run down and catch a fowl so my mother could cook her Sunday lunch. It was fun for the children to watch and help my father catch the rooster. He would throw the feed and we would circle around the fowl and grab it. My father would then kill the fowl, pluck the feathers and clean it; my mother would then season it and do the cooking. Sometimes, we would buy pork from the neighbor or a relative who killed and sold pigs on some weekends.

We usually had a full-course meal and everyone gathered around the table to enjoy my mother's best cooking. I especially enjoyed stew chicken and stew pork with rice and callaloo and ripe plantain on the side. When my older siblings were there, I would get a chicken wing while they got the legs and other meaty parts; my father would take the thigh. My mother always took the neck and the liver.

We would have our famous mauby drinks, made from the mauby tree bark that my mother soaked the night before; on other occasions we would drink the country's Ginger-beer that my mother also soaked the night before from the ginger root from my father's garden. After our delicious Sunday dinner, we had our Sunday special dessert, which was our homemade coconut ice cream. My father grated the coconut and my mother mixed the cream. The children took turns by churning the ice cream pail until the ice cream was good enough to eat.

During the week, lunch for us was mother's home-made soup with fresh vegetables such as green figs, moko, yam, cassava or plantain that my father had harvested from his garden. Some of us did not like some of the vegetables so she would make corn or plain dumplings to ensure that everyone in the family was satisfied.

One day each week, mother would cook fish stew or fried fish. She served it with rice or "ground provision" (vegetables) and sometimes with plantain and callaloo on the side. Sometimes, she would also serve the stew fish over "coo coo", which is made with corn meal and was also a favorite Island dish.

Mother bought her fish from the local fishermen in the village. Most of them were fishermen by trade. Some stayed in the Junction near to the sea and sold their fish and other seafood. There was a lot of traffic going through Claxton Bay Junction. It was the main road with cars and trucks going to and from the North, mainly Port of Spain, to San Fernando in the South. At the Junction, people waited in lines to buy oysters and pepper sauce and sometimes the cooked shrimp that was smoking on the coal-pots.

Some of the villagers lived too far into the country, so they could not go to the Junction or the market to buy their fish, so the fishermen came to them about three times a week and everyone knew the time they were supposed to drive through the village. The children would look out for the fish truck which would drive up the road. The fisherman would blow his motor horn continuously so that people who lived away from the road would know that the fisherman was coming.

Mother would get her favorite King Fish. One big fish would feed our family. It was enough for all of us to get a slice and my mother always took the head or the tail. Another was the herring fish which averaged three inches long. We called it "frydry" because when it's fried, it looks dry and you can eat the whole fish in one or two bites including the head and tail. The carite (Spanish mackerel) was another favorite of ours. My favorite dessert was coconut tart (pie), which mother baked on Saturdays along with her sweetbreads (raisin bread), multicolor cakes and the sugar cake which was made on the fireside in a pot. On special occasions, she would make currant roll or coconut tart.

Every morning we had breakfast. A normal breakfast for us on Sundays was Mother's baked bread that she made in the oven, eggs that my father fetched from the fowl coop, and some type of meat on the side, mainly pudding (sausage). We also got about two slices of sweetbread which was again my favorite. By Tuesday or Wednesday, all of our bread was finished, and so we had "bake" (flat bread) fried with salt fish, smoked-herring or just "bake" that was made on the baking stone with butter or guava jelly. Every morning, if my mother could not mix the flour to make us "bake" for breakfast, then my father would do it before going to the garden. She would put it on the baking stone and cook it on the coal-pot.

At that time, there was no electricity in many of the homes on the Island, especially in the country areas. People used wood and charcoal for cooking. The charcoal was used for burning in coal-pots. The coal-pot gave out good heat and only little flames. It was also used to make the "bake," which was placed on a baking stone on slow fire. The coal-pot was also used for heating a heavy iron that was used to iron clothes. Most people had more than one iron, so while they were using one, the other would be heating up.

The fireside was outside of the home. It was built in the outdoor kitchen next to the home. The fireside was used for cooking big meals because it took a lot of wood and gave out more smoke and heat than the coal-pot; therefore, a larger pot or pan was used for cooking.

Mother would have a cup of coffee every morning but she would make us tea with vervine leaf or young lime tree leaves from our garden. She also gave us hot cocoa that she grated from the cocoa block which was made from a relative's cocoa tree. My mother had a cabinet with beautiful china dishes and tea sets which she got as gifts from her wedding. She used them only on special occasions, so my father bought enamel cups for everyday use. They had the bigger enamel cups and we, the children, got to drink from smaller ones. We had fresh milk from our cows and fresh juice that my father made with oranges or grapefruits from the kitchen garden.

CHAPTER 13: FARMING

By summer it was crop-time and the farmers were ready to take their sugar cane to Forres Park Factory which was about two miles from Union Village. The farmers from the surrounding villages also took their cane there, had it weighed and got paid by the weight. My father took about four loads a day to the mill. He could not afford to pay a helper, so most times he asked us to help him load the cart before and after school.

Our mule, Madeline, was my father's bread-and-butter. He depended on her to take his crop to the mill. She was a faithful laborer and my father's biggest joy. My father had planted a lot of sugar cane so he needed a strong mule or bull to pull the cart and carry his crop to the sugarcane factory.

My father said that he went to our sister island, Tobago, and bought Madeline. Her mother was a race horse and participated during the Tobago

Racing season. She was fast, strong, and loved to play. Sometimes she would burst her rope and run up the road. My cousins or neighboring friends would come to tell my father that Madeline broke her rope and gott away. We would go after her and when she saw us running, she would run like a race horse. Most of the village people knew that she was my father's mule, so they also would join in and try to stop her. Madeline was fun for everyone.

CHAPTER 14: CHORES

I was older now and my father saw that I was more agile than the others, and so he always asked for my help in the field most of the time. The younger children now were older too, so they assisted with the lighter chores, like cleaning the house, sweeping the yard and bringing water from the roadside standpipe for mother to wash and fill the Goblet for drinking. The roadside standpipe was a free public water supply that was only on main roads in communities. People would line up to collect water for their cooking, washing, bathing or other household chores. The standpipes are still in some country areas today.

We all had chores to do before we went to school or play. My first job at the time was to sweep the house every morning and help with the dishes. Sometimes, I brought water from the standpipe across the street for my mother to wash. As we grew older, we were given more chores to do.

Boy getting water from standpipe

At this time my eldest sister, Petty, went out to do living-in work. I was then the oldest sibling at home so my chores became heavy. I never complained; it was a normal routine for everyone. My mother used to be ill many times with fever, so my father helped by making breakfast for us before he went to the field. My father was also a good cook. He made us fresh eggs that he picked up from the fowl coop early in the morning together with his fried bake. He would make us "bush tea" (vervine leaf was his favorite) with fresh cow's milk. On many occasions, I helped him milk the cow. When I became competent at milking the cow, it also became one of my daily chores.

When Papa, my paternal grandfather died, my father was still a teenager. As the only boy in the house, he took over Papa's jobs of working in the fields and doing the gardening. He used his father's energy and began planting lots of vegetables and fruits to supplement the sugarcane, since fruits were grown in estates scattered throughout the less inhabited areas of the country. Our land had yams, cassava, plantains, bananas, coconuts, sapodilla, cashima, soursop, oranges and other types of tropical fruit trees. On weekends, my father would gather his produce and take them to the market to sell. He used the proceeds to buy groceries to feed his family for the week.

We, the younger children, looked forward to our father coming home from the market on Sundays because we all got a penny allowance. Most of the times, mainly after lunch, we would go to our cousin Tinan's parlor "store" to buy a penny snowball or bread and pepper, which was the favorite for most of the kids in the village. Cousin Tinan was a short brown-skinned, middle-aged lady who treated all the kids in the village like we were her own, and she would always ask us about our mother and father and how they were doing and to say hello to them. Like most of the older people Cousin Tinan believed in the old days. Whenever she ironed, she would not go near the icebox, so she would ask the older kids to shave their own snowball, which was fun for them because they got to shave more ice for themselves.

Cousin Tinan had passed on and it was not long before another parlor store opened up about two houses across the street from our house. This parlor was owned by an East Indian lady named Manbass and her husband who everyone called Babu. Manbass was a friend of my parents and lived on a floor above the parlor. She was around middle age at the time and she always wore a Sari outfit, mainly white with a nylon scarf thrown over her shoulder. Babu sometimes wore a white vest and short khaki pants. He helped out with the heavier work in the store. Manbass was known by everyone in the village and always knew who we were. Like cousin Tinan, she always asked about our parents and would say, "Tell them howdy for me, eh?"

Of course as the children grew older, our parents did not have to go to the store. They gave us a list to buy whatever they needed--which was not much since we grew most of our food and my father bought some of his meat from the market after selling his produce.

CHAPTER 15:
HOUSE WIFE

While we were at school, my mother would care for the younger children at home and prepare lunch for all of us. She always made time for herself during the day. In her spare time she would make sure to listen to her favorite and only story on the radio, "None So Blind." It was a love story. Scott was a blind young handsome gentleman. A young lady by the name of Jenny (I believe) was in love with him. Since most people in the country did not have television in those days, everyone who had a radio would listen to "None So Blind", a favorite in the country. Everyone-men, women, girls, and even boys-glued themselves to their radios when that story came on.

My mother would also get her sewing machine out and start sewing for her children or crocheting a doily for the table, while listening to the news on the radio. Most people in the village did not have to go to the stores to buy clothing material. Once a week, a Syrian gentleman walked house to house with bolts of cloth to sell to the villagers. The village people called him "The Syrian." He was white and from Lebanon. My mother was one of his favorite customers and she waited for him every week. She told him what material she wanted and each week she paid him some money until he was paid in full.

CHAPTER 16: "THE HOUSE SPOT" IN CARATAL

My grandfather's house in Caratal was no longer there. My father took it down and got everything that he could use to help build his new house in Union Village. That piece of land was then left empty so it was called and continued to be called "The House Spot". My father now had to walk to his garden or get transportation to go to his old home location, so he saved money and bought a bicycle to ride to work and visit the House Spot.

He spent most of the day at the garden cleaning and planting and came back late in the evening. This was okay with my mother because she was near her kinfolks, her mother and one of her sisters, since our two-room home was an additionn to theirs and

51

she always had food on the table, some of which my father had brought.

It was like snacks for us when my father brought us and our cousins the fruits that were in season, especially mangoes. We could not wait for him to come home. Sometimes, we would even tell our friends to come over to get some mangoes, all from my father's garden. My father kept working in the fields to support his family, which increased to nine children. He now had enough money saved up so he rented a parcel of church land a few yards from my grandmother's house, and there he built our house which is still standing today.

CHAPTER 17: PETS

At our new location we had lots of animals such as goats, pigs and cattle. We also had fowls. My mother always had a cat that stayed inside the house. She would say that the cat keeps the mice away. She called all our cats "Pussycat." We once had a beautiful grey and black cat. Pussycat, as she was called, was very intelligent and playful. Mother fed her everyday and she was fat and fluffy.

One night, I woke up and went to my mother's room and saw Pussycat just there staring at me. It was the first time that I saw the eyes of a cat like a light to the room, and I got so scared that I screamed. Pussycat just said "meow" and ran under the bed. Ever since then, I never liked cats, especially in the house.

Then there were the dogs that stayed outside as guards. The dogs alerted us when someone was approaching the house. We knew when a stranger was coming because the dogs would continue to bark.

My youngest brother, Nicho, had his own goat that he took care of. When it had young ones, my father sold them and gave all the money to Nicho.

We also got proceeds from selling some of our pigs. At Christmas time we would kill one of our male pigs, sell some of the meat, share some with relatives and friends in the village, and still have enough for us to eat. Every part of the pig was used, including the feet from which souse was made. The guts were washed thoroughly and turned over on the wrong side to make tripe. The tripe was then filled with blood from the pig and seasoning added to make black pudding which was part of the Sunday morning breakfast. Left-over food was always given to the animals.

CHAPTER 18:
RELATIVES

When one of my mother's sisters died, she left three children (one boy and two girls), so my grandmother and her daughter, "Nen," who lived with her, decided to raise the young girls Margaret and Rita while the boy went to live with his father. Rita, the older daughter, was very pretty and much older than us, but she looked younger than her age. She was always well-dressed and on the go and so she remained an idol in my mind. I can remember saying how pretty and stylish she was and I would like to look like her when I get older.

We all~my aunt's four boys, her two nieces, and my mother's four girls and four boys~resided together in our little but always comfortable house in Union Village. I loved our house and enjoyed going over the little board (the bar that separated the two houses) to my grandmother's house to see Ma-me-me, my Aunt Nen and cousins.

CHAPTER 19:
MA-ME-ME

When I was of age, my grandmother would have me comb her hair and sometimes massage her. She would always have a piece of sugar cake or something sweet that she would give to me. If I said "No thanks, Ma," she would say "Take it, child." Even today, I still have that sweet tooth and still long for my grandmother's sugar cake. She was warm and had a rare strength in her, and most family members sought her advice and learned from her wisdom.

Ma-me-me always told us stories. When it started to rain and the sun was out at the same time, she would say:

"Sun and rain,
monkey maridin (marrying)"
OR

> *"Crick crack,*
> *monkey break me back*
> *for a piece of pomerac (fruit)"*

She would also tell us that if you throw anything outside of the house after dark, you must say:

> *"Dusk, excuse me."*

She gave me the name "Yangoo," meaning nice child. My Grandmother was not superstitious, but she believed in the old-fashioned ways. When someone sneezed, she would say "blessem." At that time, I never knew that she meant "bless you". When someone died and their funeral passed by the house, she would throw a cup of water and say "Blessem" and close the door until the funeral procession passed.

Funeral processions in those days were very long. Since there were just one or two cars in the village, everyone had to walk behind the hearse from the dead persons house until they reached the church or cemetery for burial. It was traditional that when someone died, there would be a wake every night until the day of the funeral. It was like a celebration. Some families would hurriedly build a tent on the side or front of their house to accommodate everyone during this period. Sometimes, the body would be in the house on ice, according to the person's wish or it may be at the funeral home.

The older women stayed in the house singing their favorite hymns, according to their religion, and praying. The older men played cards and games and again, according to the deceased's religion, there would be drumming and dancing of different forms like the limbo. Very few of the wakes had bamboo bursting and stick fighting, since these were older traditions. Bursting a bamboo required putting some kerosene in one of the gutted sections, then passing a flambeau (lighted cloth at the end of a bottle containing kerosene) at the end of the bamboo. This would cause the bamboo to make a loud noise like a gunshot. Hot, black coffee, biscuit and cheese or light foods were served during a wake to everyone who wanted. The younger people played games outside of the house and participated in some of the events.

CHAPTER 20: NEN AND TANTY BAKING

Our kitchen was built flat on the ground and about ten feet from the house. It was covered with carat leaves and was about twelve square feet with a door on the side and another to the front. There were two firesides. For cooking, my aunt Nen had her own space and my mother used the other. There was one big oven adjacent to one of the firesides. This was built with brick and sand; it had one door in the front and a window on the side.

Both families shared the same oven by baking on the weekends. On Saturdays, they would knead their flour and put it out to rise in their home-made bread pan. Sometimes my mother would make her multicolor cake by mixing butter with the Island's coarse sugar until it was soft enough to put in the flour and other ingredients.

Lady Baking

My father would chop the wood to size and light the oven. When the oven was hot and ready for baking, the women would put in their dough. After about an hour, when the bread had a light golden color, they knew it was done. The bread was fluffy and we all enjoyed eating it. "It was the best bread I have ever eaten." My mother and my aunt Nen usually made their sweetbreads (raisin breads) and coconut tarts (pies) and drops (like cupcakes) while we the older children helped by grating coconuts, shelling corn or just watching while the two mothers made their sugar cakes on the firesides or cooked their delicious foods.

They always started baking earlier in the day because most of us had to either play or practice some type of sport on Saturday evenings. When my grandmother was stronger, she would cook her favorite accra and saltfish, a dry fish that is sold mostly in the Caribbean, and prepare her delicious pound plantain, which everyone enjoyed. Our grandmother taught us how to pound the plantain (banana family) in a wooden pot called a mortar, using a pestle, a wooden tool resembling a small baseball bat. Sometimes we took turns with our cousins to pound the plantain.

CHAPTER 21:
FUN TIMES

Boys were allowed to go to the bush to hunt or to the beach for sea bathing. They would take their home-made slingshots and their pen knives with them. They would return with wild meat such as iguana. When they went to the beach, they would bring back crabs, conchs, and/or oysters. My mother used to season the meat and either curried or stewed it. It was very tasty to us at the time. My brothers and their friends would come around with beverages and they all enjoyed the wild meat while they "limed" (gathered around, "old-talking") on the square.

Girls were never allowed to go hunting or sea bathing with boys. My mother said that we were young ladies and had no right to be in the bush or on the beach with the young boys.

At home, I would stay around my brothers and their friends and listen to them "old talk" or watch them play cards. When they were not gathering at our house, they would be on my grandmother's gallery (porch) where everyone was welcome.

We all had our play-time. While my brothers and their friends pitched marbles, rode their home-made scooters, or used bats to roll tires down the hill, the older boys played cricket or table tennis (ping-pong). The girls played hop-scotch, rounders (similar to basketball), jump rope or "needle and thread." Sometimes if our parents allowed us, we would play "egg and spoon," running with boiled eggs in a spoon. If the boys allowed us, sometimes we would join in with them while they played the "bag race" (hopping in sacks) down the hill from our house.

Sometimes we played "house" in the bushes near our parents' house. We also played parents and teachers and on one occasion we had a real funeral when we buried a dead bird. That was very sad. There were no street lights in our village so the kids had to be in the house before it got dark, usually around 6.30 pm. We looked forward for full moons because the nights would be bright and we could stay outside later. Our favorite games on a moonlight night were hopscotch or skip—jumping rope to the song:

"In and out the dusty bluebells..."

CHAPTER 22: COUSINS

My grandmother had nine beautiful daughters. Some of her daughters were married to men outside of their race and religion, so her grandchildren included Spanish, Caucasian, Indian and Chinese.

Since we lived near our grandmother, we got to see all of our aunts and cousins who were my mother's sisters, nieces and nephews. My mother was the last of her mother's nine daughters, so most of her nephews and nieces were close to her age and some even had children of their own. Most of them had large families and they all came to see Ma-me-me, who was a great-grandmother by that time.

There was another niece who I admired whenever she visited us. She came very often and would always bring her three boys with her. Cousin

Verona was flashy and never looked her age, and even today she still looks stylish. I used to admire her and Rita because of the way they dressed, always looking as young and fashionable.

Older Generation

New Generation

CHAPTER 23:
OUR NEW HOUSE

My father had saved up enough money to build a bigger house for his family which was increasing in size. He rented a piece of land from the Anglican Church a little further away from Ma-me-me and built a house on a little hill. Our new house was roofed with galvanized tin that my father bought from the hardware store. He used cedar wood from the trees that he had planted on his land in previous years to make the inside walls. After cutting down the trees, large portions were taken by truck to a factory to be cut into boards.

Our new house

The house had three bedrooms, a living/dining area, one bathroom, a big eat-in kitchen and an open basement. Our house was well furnished with the latest Morris chairs with beautiful colored cushions and a wooden dining table with four chairs. This set was made by one of the local carpenters in the village. My mother had a beautiful canopy over her four-poster bed that was always well made up whenever anyone entered her bedroom.

There were no telephones in the village at that time. When my brothers wanted to get together with friends who lived nearby, or with our cousins in the front house, they would whistle for one another. My cousins often came to the back at our house and we went to the front to their house. I never learned to whistle, although I tried.

In later years, my grandmother became very old and physically weak and could no longer visit us or any of her other children. She stayed in her room most of the time. Everyday, my aunt Nen came to our house to visit and brought a plate of her delicious food, and my mother also gave her some of her food. They cooked every day for their families. Sometimes Nen would spend hours at our house and they would talk "patois" (broken French), and when any of the children would get between them or they thought that we were listening, they would tell us to leave and not get into big people's business.

Sometimes, they would even dance to the radio music when they heard an old calypso of their liking. My mother and her sister Nen were always happy together and would share that joy with their other sister, Aunty Cyril, or other sisters when either of them came to visit.

My mother taught us some of her songs, like:

Maybell my dear, mother send you to school
To learn to read and write.
So Maybell, I want you to stand on the spot
And spell me the word Maybell.
Maybell said:
May is may and mother, Bell is bell
Mother said:
That's not the way my child.
May is the 5 (fifth) month of the year and Bell
is a thing that you ring.

Another of my favorite songs was:
When I was just a little girl,
I asked my mother
What will I be,
will I be happy,
will I be sad?
Here's what she said to me:
Que Sera, Sera;
whatever will be, will be
The future's not ours to see;
Que Sera, Sera

My mother and her sister Nen had the most beautiful voices.

CHAPTER 24:
MY BROTHERS

My brothers always had their friends over to our house. Now older and no longer interested in going to the bush to hunt, or going to the sea to catch crabs or oysters, my brothers decided to build a tennis (ping-pong) table underneath our house. There they and their friends would practice when they did not have football (soccer), cricket or basketball. Table tennis was a fun game for everyone and by looking at the boys play, I learned the game. After a few months of practice with my brothers, I got good at it and even won against them sometimes. I learned to love table tennis and played at every opportunity that I got.

My eldest brother, Rupert, was living and attending school in the city of Port-of-Spain and visited us in the summer, once a year, so my mother would bake her gourmet dishes for his arrival.

Days before he came home, all my cousins would get excited and come to our house and talk about him. On the day of his arrival, my older cousin Prowler and some of my other kin-folks would go about a quarter of a mile down the road, as far as the bridge, to meet our big brother who came on the train to Claxton Bay and then walked home to Union Village.

Our brother was the only child in the village who wore glasses at the time. Since he was coming from the City and was attending Fatima College, one of the highest learning institutions, everyone respected him. He had the appearance of a handsome, well-educated young gentleman with his "grip" (suitcase) and his glasses. Rupert was very gentle, and since childhood had been nicknamed "Gentle." He never stayed with us for more than a week or two; my mother would say that if he did stay long, he would never want to leave.

Rupert continued his education in the City and after graduation, when his godmother (stepmother) had died, my mother sent my father to get him because his stepfather had remarried. Gentle was now home with us in Union Village and became popular with the fellas (boys). He joined the different sports clubs in the village and became good in every sport.

CHAPTER 25:
LIMERS BOYS

All my brothers and most of my cousins in the village played sports. They played basketball, soccer and cricket. They entered many competitions and played against the other villages and counties. Limers Club was their group name. The name Limers came up since most of the young men in the village would gather by the trace (street-corner) near my grandmother's house, to have meetings, discuss sports and news, and give each other "fatigue" (tell jokes). They still do this today when those of the older generation get together. Since we lived in a multiracial community, Limers Club members included both East Indians and Negroes. The Club's annual dance was always a large success with patrons coming from different parts of the island and I looked forward to that and all of the other activities.

Limers boys

We did not wear cheerleader uniforms, but whenever Limers boys played, I would do my chores early so I could go to their games to join with others in cheering and supporting them. Most of our female cousins would be right there on the lines also cheering them on. Everyone in the village knew when Limers boys had to play basketball, cricket or football. We were all excited about their games. They were good players and won most of their matches. My cousin Prowler was one of the best local goalkeepers in the South of the island and my brothers were good also.

Their playing field was in the Savannah just across the river (canal) and about half a mile from our house. My father had thrown a log, as a bridge, from one side of the river to the other. This was a short cut for everyone. It saved us from walking an extra mile to the savannah or spring, as the field was called. None of us had ever thought about falling off the log and drowning in the water, which was about three feet deep. If I was late for a game, I would run over that log and be at the Savannah in minutes. Sometimes the river would overflow and cover the log, but we would feel for it and jump over to the other side of the river bank.

When we could not go over the banks, then we would go the long way, up the road and take the trace near the Wildman's to the savannah. Even though they lived near to the field, I never heard the Wildmans complain about the noise or of any disturbances that went on during the games. Errol, "Cheesy", was also in Limers club, so it was a pleasure going past their home and other club members' family homes on our way to the field.

CHAPTER 26:
LIMERS DANCE

Limers Club often gave dances (parties) to raise money to buy their sporting equipment. The parties were always grand. Since one of my brothers was a policeman working in Port of Spain, he had some friends who came to the dances all the way from the city. I remember two sisters who also became our friends and sometimes slept over at our house, and my mother would cook breakfast for them. Today, Marina and Jean, who remain close family friends, still remember my mother's cooking. My mother never objected to me or my sister going to the dances because my brothers and cousins would be there. She knew they would look out for us.

My brother would give some money to my older sister and we would go shopping to buy materials to make our own dresses. First we would go to the stores and look at the new styles in the window.

We would then come home and make our own clothes, which were always outstanding. Since I was a member of Limers Club, I was always asked to help out when there was a dance. I would volunteer to work at the door or at the bar so that I could meet people.

CHAPTER 27: YOU KNOW YOU CAN DANCE

I learned to dance with the club members. Some of them were too shy and young to dance with strangers but they would dance with their club members. My cousin Prowler was also a great dancer and he showed his colors especially when he was dancing with his partner who was also a club member by the name of Lyris. They were the dancing King and Queen on the floor. When they danced, everyone stood and watched. We had slow dances like the waltz and foxtrot. We also did the bounce and other old dances that our mothers had showed us.

CHAPTER 28: OVER THE YEARS

Some of the village children have since moved away to other countries and others are married and have children and grandchildren of their own. The elders have passed but they have left with us a rare strength that I will always cherish. They were all so warm and thought us simple things. What we learned from them is certainly History that was not yet written in books but stories passed down orally from generation to generation. We learned to respect the past and our own heritage.

Our house that was always full of joy and laughter with so many children, relatives and friends, is still standing. It has been renovated many times and it now has a modern look with an indoor bathroom, a washing machine and even air-conditioning. Maybe in the near future, we might get a dishwasher and a dryer. In the meantime, we would enjoy drying our clothes on the clothesline with natural heat from the sun.

My grandmother's house is not there anymore, but my cousin Prowler built his house on the spot that her house was on. My other cousins, Charlo, Sub, Max, Knolly and some of our other relatives helped to make the blocks and build his house. Prowler is deceased now, but his wife, Gracie, and some of their children are still there. Like ours, their house has been renovated and decorated with all the modern appliances.

We had one love for each other then, and today, everyone has grown up and times have changed, but that love is still there.

◆　　◆　　◆　　◆　　◆　　◆

Looking back over the years,

I have learned to appreciate

"My life in Trinidad

as I remember it."

Through my parents' struggle

On their long journey,

I admired them

how they stayed strong to the end

◆　　◆　　◆　　◆　　◆　　◆

EPILOGUE

My life now has changed tremendously. I reside permanently in the United States of America and my children have all grown up. My parents are deceased and most of my kin folks are here in the United States. I have nieces and nephews here in Washington, DC; Queens, N.Y.; Atlanta, GA; Baltimore, MD; Chicago, IL and London, England. Because the family has scattered all over the world, we all try to go to the Family Reunion in Trinidad, the birth of our ancestors, every three years so we can get acquainted with the rest of the Family and the younger children could meet their aunts; uncles and cousins. The Reunion gives the younger generation a sense of family and hope and an insight of how far their parents have come. It's also a way for them to see a different part of the world and hope that they can be inspired by the experience.

The older people used to say, "Wisdom comes with age and with it comes knowl- edge". Now that I am older, I have become wiser and more knowledgable. I have traveled to many places while living here in the United States. One of my most memo- rable trips was my visit to Rome, Italy. Traveling to Rome with the Honors group of the History department where I work made it more memorable because the students were there to learn the history of the Romans. For me, it was an educa- tional and also a spiritual journey. Just standing on the same ground on which Jesus was crucified and going to mass at St. Peter's Shrine where Pope John Paul II gave his Sermon, was inspiring. Some call it the Vatican City or Holy City or St. Peters Basilica Cathedral of Rome because St. Peter was buried there. It was a joy for me just standing in the circled Square with so many people of different races and culture all waiting to hear and see the Pope from his window a few stories up in the building. From the square, you can see the structure of the church with it's giant marble columns and in front of and at the top of the columns are statues of the disciples. Also mounted in the front is the statue of St.Peter. I was also reminded of the Biblical movies that we see every Easter when we visited the ancient Shrine and the Platform where the pirates fought.

Sometimes, I still have visions of growing up and seeing my Father working in the cane fields and riding his bicycle to his vegetable garden, saying hello to everyone that he sees on the way. I still have thoughts of my mother and her sister talking in their second language and me combing my grandmother's hair.

My memories as a child in the land that I grew up are not the same anymore, so I must now let go and live my dreams and hopes not just of the past but of the present and future.